The Quigmans

by Buddy Hickerson

Harmony Books ‹○○› New York

Published by Harmony Books, 201 East 50th Street, New York, New York 10022. Member of the Crown Publishing Group.

HARMONY and colophon are trademarks of Crown Publishers, Inc.

Manufactured in the United States of America

Library of Congress Cataloging-in-Publication Data
Hickerson, Buddy.
    The quigmans / by Buddy Hickerson. — 1st ed.
      p. cm.
    1. American wit and humor, Pictorial. I. Title.
NC1429.H48A4 1990
741.5′973—dc20   90-4755
                         CIP

ISBN 0-517-58023-3

10 9 8 7 6 5 4 3 2 1

First Edition

Special thanks to Shirley, who appears twice in this book.

This book is dedicated to anyone who buys it.

Notice: If you happen to see an occasional "⌧" beside the signature of Buddy Hickerson, do not panic. This merely denotes a Quigman who was written by his collaborator, Mike Stanfill, a creature of pinkish hue and neurotic demeanor.

For those within whom the urge wells up, direct all correspondence to: Quigland, 2330 Jonesboro, Dallas, Texas 75228.

Thank you, The Management.

The Quigmans

Upon retiring after 40 years of service,
Bob receives a complimentary brick.

"Gee, Francine. You eat like a bird."

Encumbered by a low self-image, Bob takes a job as a speed bump.

"Bad dog! BAD DOG! You don't wear pearls with plaid! CRETIN!"

"I told you an unfixed male cat will spray."

"Yes, ladies and gentlemen . . . It looks as though Bob has taken an early lead in the middle-aged men's downhill race."

"Oh, Jowles . . . I hate to spoil the romantic mood, but have you been fixed?"

"What aisle's the toast on?"

"Nice carpet, Mr. Quigman. Wouldn't want
to see anything happen to it.
Now WOULD we?"

At the beach, women would dress Bob
with their eyes.

"Oh, Bob! That's your sixth bottle. I just
ADORE an Aqua Velva man!"

Moe's evening was ruined when his date
made it known that she too would like
something to eat.

"Take the pain, Marcie. You can still shop on this leg. Let's ambush that skirt sale!"

"Marcie! Get that dog off the table! He's using the wrong fork!"

"Watch out for Heimlich. That guy
can maneuver!"

"I thought you'd like it . . . It's my new perfume made from 17 herbs and spices."

"Gimme the money, lady . . . or I tell everyone you had an affair with ME, the ugliest guy in the world! YAHAHAHAHA!"

"Yessiree!! That No-Guest Strip really
works wonders, Hon."

Avant Guard Dog

A chilling scene from *The Elephant Dog*.

McComedy.

Bob prepares to embark on a guilt trip.

"That suit really matches your eyes."

"I'd like a big ol' juicy cheeseburger. But
hold the meat and stick some
yogurt in there."

Moses of the Left Lane-ites.

"Oops! Looks like Barbie and Ken stayed
in the sauna too long."

"Well . . . It's our first date. How does dinner, movie, and a blood test sound?"

Miraculously, and just as he had wished, Enid Kronkman was visited by the I.Q. fairy.

"We've gotta get off this planet FAST! I've never felt so . . . USED!!"

"So, Mr. Rubble . . . Your latent insecurity relates proportionately to your shame in being a cartoon character with big, goofy feet."

Sasha's love affair with health food and
cleanliness became a reckless obsession
when she began guzzling
wheat germ shampoo.

"MAN OVERDRAWN!!"

"Then, when you're thirteen . . . a mysterious thing happens once a month, Shirley. . . . You begin to receive a MasterCard bill."

"HEY! Quit ringin' those phones! Whatsa matter with you people out there? Don't you not care enough to help?"

"I dunno, Cowboy Bob. . . . I never liked pierced ears on a man."

Due to a slippage in the "Quigmans" ratings, I'd like to introduce a NEW CHARACTER today....He's CUDDLES, the irresistible PUPPY with Big, Moist eyes!

OMIGOD!

AAAAH!

hickerson

"Ward! I need to talk to you about the human!"

"Hey! Where is everybody?"

PSYCHOANALYSIS RESTAURANT

Menu:
Repressed Duck ——— 25.00
Fillet of Sole Searching ~ 24.50
Shrimp Basket Case ——— 28.00
Self Expresso ——— 3.00
Banana Split Personality ——— 6.50
Strawberry Shortcomings ——— 4.00

hickerson

Bob suffers the heartbreak of visible
boxer-short lines.

"Hey, kids! Whaddaya say we go out, get ourselves a few devil tattoos, and ride to Frisco with Hell's Angels?"

"As you can see, I live in a very fashionable neighborhood."

Bob suffers elevator lag.

Poorly planned diner holdup.

"Well . . . the Dodge is crunchier . . . chomp, chomp . . . but the Ford—gulp—is more pleasing to the palate."

To keep his ego intact, Bob imagined he was wearing "female block."

"No, NO, Bob! I believe you have the
instructions confused with those
of the harmonica!"

"Oh, Bob . . . I just adore the strong, silent, absorbent, scuff-resistant type."

"I dunno, Doc! Every now and then this hat and stuff just SHOW UP."

"You called at a bad time,
Bob . . . the '90s!"

The Crime Channel.

"Other people's leftovers for me, and she'll have the same."

"Hello. Do I know me? That's why I carry Amnesia Express!"

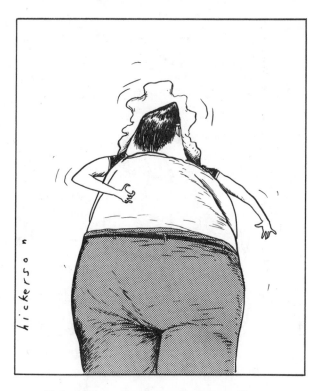

Bob was so nervous, he bit someone
ELSE's lip.

"Here ya go, kids . . . EMPTY Popsicle
sticks! YAHAHAHAHA!!!"

Donald Trump on "Hullaballoo."

Madge Levine: Jungle Cosmetologist.

"Honey! Could I get an entrée with this?"

"Now, General Barksider . . . Here's my proposal . . . Will you marry me?"

"You're a nice guy, Butch. And I'm glad you've never had a disease, but you also seem to be immune to the germ of an idea."

Feeding time for the balloon animals.

Writers' strike.

"You're no Dan Quayle, Bob."

"You are getting sleepy. Your eyelids are getting heavy. You will give us longer lunch hours. You will install a water cooler."

Peterson was a cop who went strictly by the book. Unfortunately, that book was *The Joy of Ballet*.

"Rudolf! I KNEW you were seeing someone else! I'm sick and tired of your reindeer games!"

"This is Nigel Vapid for MTV, reporting from the tragic aftermath of the Battle of the Bands. Sad, indeed."

"Charm bracelet, eh? Must be broken."

"I'm almost through scraping all the paint off your car. . . . You did call for a stripper, right?"

Heavyweight bout with regression.

"Look at that, Clyde! She's playin' hard to fathom!"

Bob's day includes a Power Breakfast, Power Massage, Power Walk, Powering up his P.C., Power Meetings, Power Lunch, and listening to some Tower of Power... but thank God he's rechargeable!

"Don't get me wrong, Helga. . . . I love
quiet girls. . . . I just get the feeling you
look at other men the same way
you look at me!"

Bob attempts to get high on himself.

The Drug Czar Gourmet.

"Whaddaya MEAN, your hot water doesn't work? . . . GET REAL! I got a planet to save, Bucko!"

Bob suffers the greenhouse effect.

"Yes, YES! She's got him where she
wants him. An irreversible WEDLOCK!
Ooo! That's gotta hurt."

"Stop me if I'm off base, here, but . . . you
could use a good massage!"

"I LOVE the American people. . . . I had several for lunch today. HA.HA.HA. The liberals gave me indigestion! Their knees kept jerking! HA.HA.HA. . . . but seriously. . . ."

Bob kept finding proof that he was, indeed, an island.

Rajneesh Dangerfield.

"I'm lookin' for the man who shot
my paw!"

The New Marines strive to make boot
camp a kinder place.

Francine outlines her wedding plans.

Nurse Floyd possessed the rare ability
to turn a man's head . . . and
make him cough.

"Take this tie with you, Sir Myron. It will ward off good taste."

Francine was a morning person.

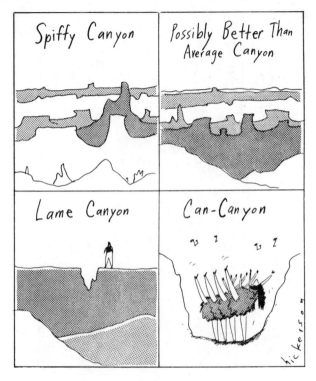

Grand Canyon alternatives.

Environmental archeologists.

"I don't want to embarrass you, Francine, but . . . you have something in your teeth."

"SHUT UP!! It's not my fault I lost the case! It's YOUR fault, you PIG!! NYAA! NYAA! NYAAA!!"

"Run for your lives!! He's heavily armed!"

"I figured it out, Billy. Parents are probation officers with food."

When investors break up.

Shirley possessed a Turbo Charge Card.

"Sorry. We're closed. Sold out years ago."

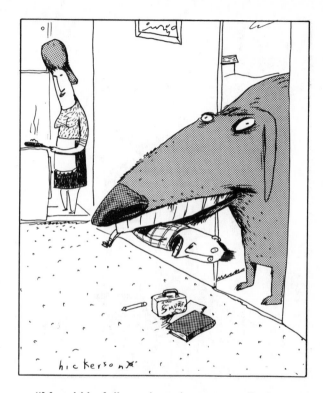

"Mom! He followed me home. . . . Do we have to keep him?"

Shortly after having her legs waxed,
Francine experiences the heartbreak of
waxy yellow build-up.

As a child, Bob had obviously teethed
too long.

"Pull over, lady! You're exceeding your credit limit!"

Bob finally gets into shape. Unfortunately,
it is the shape of a giant zucchini squash.

"Lemme guess. . . . You were a test-tube baby, right?"

"Join me in a beer?"

Bob suspected women only liked him for
his hair's body.

"Beatrice, you know I've been happily
married to Sylvia for many years . . . but
I always think of you as the one
that got away."

"Not now, Jowles. Just because I have a
biological clock doesn't mean I'm
open 24 hours."

"I don't like her friends, she doesn't like
my friends, and frankly, Doc . . .
we're starving!"

"Francine! Have you seen my flare gun?"

"Damn this jungle! Now Figby's got it! I
give him three weeks and he'll be sharing
the spotlight with Adrian Zmed!"

"Lil' Jocko and his father haven't spoken
to each other in years. . . . I'm so
proud of them."

Various rappers.

"Hi, Stan. I'm Edna. Francine said to tell you she's sick of playing dumb for you, and she paid me to be your surrogate mindless subhuman chattel."

Hugh Hefner Orders a Hit!

The Platonic Verses

by Bob Quigman

"Bob Quigman has shamed all that is male with the release of his pathetic dating memoirs. I'm having him killed."

Bob's girlfriend thanked the doctor for all
he had done.

"Hey! That ad was no lie: 'An equestrian-
style ranch home with a distinct New
England flavor.' "

"Remember, girls . . . We're gonna strike
fast and strike hard. Synchronize your
biological clocks and follow me!"

"Hey! They're burning Atlanta! Anybody
got marshmallows?"

"Hello, Bob! My name is Joy and these
are my sisters, Hope, Grace,
and Trauma!"

A typical episode of "Nazi Landing."

"And now . . . we'd like to introduce our choice for Puppet of the Year: The entire Chilean Parliament!"

Ayatollah Khomeini and the June Terrorist Dancers.

"No thanks, Peggy! One suburb is my limit!"

"Y'know what drives men crazy? Insanity."

Paparazzi of the Renaissance.

"Hi! I've surrounded your house with dry
kindling and a light patina of kerosene,
and a fellow campfire girl with a
matchbook is awaiting my signal.
Care to buy some cookies?"